2004
john beasley
big green
annual

£24.95

big green
annual

by john beasley

additional pictures

brian armstrong	Sad Mad Bad p.92
chris beasley	General Confusion p.66
chris cook	Natalie Lloyd p.58, Persona Pride p.70, Finder Keeps p.71
john grossick	Dream Of My Life p.16, Extra Jack p.17, Mozielaw p.31, Victoria's Boy p.53, Meander p.60, Imps Way p.71, Beer Tent p.71, Officials p.78, Touchez Du Bois p97, Smiles p.101, Harriet Bethell p.101, Hattie p.104, Royalecko p.112, Jo Foster p.124, Rutherford p.131, Lordberniebouffant p.152
tim holt	Inner State p.93, Ashley Farrant p.111, Rosie Booth p.112, Waiting p.156
john mullen	Dai Jones p.70, Beasley p.87, Ystradowen p.94
david strange	Cash'N'Carrots p.35, Tim Underwood p.64, Ballysicyos p.68, Novice riders p.87, Sweet Kari p.91, Gunners Mistake p.105, All Eyez On Me p.128

associate editor: david briers

design by *bobco*

printed by Lotus Press Ltd
62-64 Nuffield Road Nuffield Industrial Estate
Poole Dorset BH17 0RS
first published in Great Britain by paleface publications
30 thistlebarrow road bournemouth dorset BH7 7AL 01202 309489

the moral right of the author has been asserted

ISBN 0-9539608-3-8

big green
annual

contents

2005 fixture list	4
january	**7**
february	**25**
rosemary gasson	44
march	**55**
wish list	73
april	**91**
dick baimbridge	106
may/june	**119**
chris lawson	122
christopher sporborg	136
map and course locator	150

Cover: Red Rebel and Rowan Cope surge to the line ahead of Sheila McKenzie and Tim Lane to land the Brian Currie Ltd Mens Open race at Brafield on the Green.

2005 Point-to-Point fixtures

JANUARY

Monday 3rd
Cottenham
Sunday 9th
Larkhill
Tweseldown
Higham
Saturday 15th
Barbury Castle
Sunday 16th
Ampton
Barbury Castle
Sunday 23rd
Dunthrop
Blackforest Lodge
Cottenham
Alnwick
Saturday 29th
Larkhill
Sunday 30th
Weston Park
Market Rasen
Higham

FEBRUARY

Saturday 5th
Horseheath
Friars Haugh
Wadebridge
Sunday 6th
Chipley Park
Godstone
Thorpe Lodge
Tweseldown
Witton Castle
Saturday 12th
Chaddesley Corbett
Black Forest Lodge
Kingston Blount
Larkhill
Erw Lon
Sunday 13th
High Easter
Saturday 19th
Whitwick Manor
Duncombe Park
Charing
Buckfastleigh
Sunday 20th
Alnwick
Market Rasen
Dunthrop
Marks Tey
Weston Park
Milborne St. Andrew
Saturday 26th
Brocklesby Park
Parham
Badbury Rings
Horseheath
Holnicote
Sunday 27th
Mollington
Howick
Netherby
Great Trethew
Eyton on Severn
Bedale

MARCH

Saturday 5th
Didmarton
Ottery St Mary
Godstone
Cilwendeg
Sunday 6th
Charm Park
Higham
Wellbeck
Eaton Hall
Garnons
Larkhill
Corbridge
Saturday 12th
Llanfrynach
Friars Haugh
Brafield-on-the-Green
Detling
Whittington
Wadebridge
Sunday 13th
Charlton Horethorne
Andoversford
Garthorpe
Dalton Park
Ampton
Saturday 19th
Parham
Howick
Cottenham
Crossford
Hutton Rudby
Cothelstone
Siddington
Sunday 20th
Buckfastleigh
Mollington
Larkhill
Garnons
Brocklesbury Park
Saturday 26th
Charing
Mordon
Ystradowen
Kilworthy
Ston Easton
Sandon
Horseheath
Brampton Bryan
Kimble
Whittington
Badbury Ring
Dingley
Sunday 27th
Alnwick
Monday 28th
Aldington
Marks Tey
Trebudannon
Tranwell
Paxford
Lockinge
Blackforest Lodge
Thorpe Lodge
Lydstep
Eyton on Severn
Charm Park
Kingston St Mary
Hackwood Park
Tuesday 29th
Upton on Severn
Flagg Moor

APRIL

Saturday 2nd
Larkhill
Garthorpe
High Easter
Cilwendeg
Sunday 3rd
Little Windsor
Dalston
Great Trethew
Eaton Hall
Maisemore Park
Whitwell on the Hill
Penshurst
Saturday 9th
Higham
Llanvapley
Barbury Castle
Sunday 10th
Bedale
Friars Haugh
Tabley
Andoversford
Catsfield
Bitterley
Guilsborough
Cherry Brook
Kingston St Mary
Saturday 16th
Cottenham
Corbridge
Lifton
Charing
Badbury Rings
Chaddesley Corbett
Ystradowen
Sunday 17th
Clifton upon Dunsmore
Mollington
Alpraham
Stainton
Hackwood Park
Cothelstone
Saturday 23rd
Woodford
Flete Park
Balcormo Mains
Penshurst
Bonvilston
Brampton Bryan
Kingston Blount
Sunday 24th
Garthorpe
Little Windsor
Fakenham
Easingwold
Saturday 30th
Trebudannon
Laleston
Heslaker
Larkhill

MAY

Sunday 1st
Dingley
Mosshouses
Cold Harbour
Witton Castle
Monday 2nd
Pentreclwydau
Northaw
Cotley
Maisemore Park
Eyton-on-Severn
High Bickington
Ashorne
Aldington
Saturday 7th
Easingwold
Aspatria
Marks Tey
Bonvilston
Holnicote
Flete Park
Peper Harow
Sunday 8th
Stafford Cross
Chaddesley Corbett
Saturday 14th
Bredwardine
Garthorpe
Holnicote
Mordon
Kingston Blount
Sunday 15th
Hexham
Tabley
Lifton
Wednesday 18th
Cothelstone
Saturday 21st
Upper Sapey
Bratton Down
Sunday 22nd
Hexham
Dingley
Rhydygwern
Wednesday 25th
Larkhill
Saturday 28th
Garthorpe
Mounsy Hill Gate
Sunday 29th
Kingston Blount
Pentreclwdau
Monday 30th
Chaddesley Corbett
Bonvilston
Lifton

JUNE

Saturday 4th
Bratton Down
Trecoed
Sunday 12th
Bratton Down
Saturday 18th
Umbereigh

Course locator page 150

4

COMPETITORS and spectators from all over the country converge on Cottenham for the opening day of the 2004 season. Not for the first time, the season's initial contest sees the Sporborg colours take the honours, but that apart, the East Anglians are routed on home soil. Polly Gundry, whose dominance of the women's title is equivalent to that of Michael Schumacher in F1, gets on the scoresheet with Fertile Valley, but the most impressive winner of the day is Dusk Duel (Jane Williams) in the ladies' open. Sadly he breaks down irreparably at Barbury Castle two weeks later.

Dominic Alers-Hankey, who broke his leg in a hunting accident over a year earlier, wins on his comeback ride on Strong Tea at Larkhill, and then doubles up on  Kerstino Two, thereby beating Phil York, who had two winners at Higham, to the "first double of 2004" honour by 15 minutes.

Lambrini Mist, carrying the Amberleigh House colours of John Halewood, wins for Richard Burton at Tweseldown, where Tom Cobbler (Pippa Hall) beats the odds-on Bitofamixup. The latter's rider Jenny Gordon must have been ruing her generosity in lending a lorry to the Halls, whose vehicle had broken down soon after setting out.

At Barbury Castle, Upton Adventure scores the first of the eight victories which earn her the season's leading horse award. Ashley Farrant opens his account for the season on Lord Atterbury, later to finish third in the Grand National.

Godfrey Maundrell, left, completes a century between the flags on Rhythm King at Ampton, and Ollie Bush sends out both open winners at the Heythrop.

The weekend sees Polly Gundry, Richard Burton, Nick Kent, Ashley Farrant and Richard Woollacott all riding a double, but their achievement is eclipsed by Mark Walford, who boots home a treble at Market Rasen.

Diet tip of the week comes from 6'5" Charlie Shirley-Beavan, who has discovered that drinking vodka and coke is a better bet than beer for weight stabilisation.

Appalling conditions prevail both at Wadebridge, where Tabitha Cave lands a double, and at Larkhill, which sees eventual national novice champion Daryl Jacob steer home a brace for trainer Sally Alner.

Above: The Red Boy and Andrew Braithwaite are welcomed into the winners' enclosure after the CHHC Club Members' race at Cottenham.

Below: Crackrattle (Alan Brown), left, and Storm Forecast (Philip Andrew), centre, jump with eventual winner TicTac (Tim Eades), right, during the CA Club Members' Novice Riders' race at Cottenham.

Above: Legendary pointer Balisteros, ridden by Pauline Robson, begins his season with a long trip from Scotland to appear in the Cottenham Ladies' Open race.

Right: Jane Williams after her Ladies' Open race win on Dusk Duel on the first day of the new season at Cottenham.

Below: It's an early start but pointing enthusiasts turn out in droves at Cottenham for the opening meeting of the 2004 season.

Above: The grey Pendle Hill (Andrew Hickman) and Merry Minstrel (Andrew Sansome) lead the CHHC Club Members' race at Cottenham.

Right: Tooley Park and Andrew Sansome precede Maiden race winner Gray Knight (James Tudor) into the unsaddling enclosure at Cottenham.

Below: Fertile Valley and Polly Gundry come home ahead of the fancied Oneminutetofive (Ashley Farrant) to win the Restricted race at Cottenham.

Above: Tom Mann on Keegan Bearnais leads Milamoss (Tim Vaughan), Dolitanlad (Patrick Milling-ton, far side) and On A Full Wager (Joe Docker, striped sleeves) at the first fence in division one of the Maiden race at Tweseldown.

Below: The permanent grandstand and changing rooms form an impressive backdrop to the winners' enclosure at Tweseldown.

Above: Rhythm King and Godfrey Maundrell in action during division two of the Maiden race at Tweseldown.

Left: Marcus Gorman and Life's Work chasing the Men's Open field as a wintry shower sweeps across Tweseldown in Hampshire.

Below: Julian Pritchard and owner Laura Garrett after Titus Bramble won the Astaire & Partners Ltd Men's Open race at Tweseldown.

Above: No time for quiet reflection as Tom Cobbler (Pippa Hall), far side, and Bitofamixup (Jenny Gordon) take the water jump during the Ladies' Open race at Tweseldown.

Left: Rider Frank Buckett, lass Charlotte Moore and trainer Michael Madgwick with Sharp Seal after winning division two of the Maiden race at Tweseldown.

Above: Riders Patrick Millington, Joe Docker, Richard Burton and Mark Wall search for a way into the parade ring at Tweseldown.

Right: Steven Astaire, Tweseldown Racing Club chairman.

Below: Spectators at Tweseldown take a close look at runners in division one of the Maiden race.

Joanna Parris

Tom Dreaper

Daniel Skelton

Dominic
Alers Hankey

Above The second race about to start and traffic still arrives at the popular venue of Barbury Castle.

Opposite: Spectators enjoy the winter sunshine as the action unfolds
on the Wiltshire downs at Barbury Castle.

Below: Restricted race winner Highway Oak (Nick Mitchell), right, follows Anflora (Nick Williams) with
Cloudy Bay Boy (Rowan Cope), far side, at Barbury Castle.

Above: The grey Dream Of My Life and Ran Morgan jump with Raging Torrent (Luke Morgan) and Boulta (Tom Oates) to win the Confined race at Alnwick.

Below: Members' race winner Jo Parris and Ryans Star at Dunthrop.

Right: Upton Adventure and rider Emma James after winning a competitive Ladies' Open race sponsored by Fawcetts at Barbury Castle.

16

Above: Legal Storm and Richard Green lead the PPORA Club race for novice riders at Barbury Castle with Igloux Royal (Matthew Briggs), far side, and Boyne Banks (Guy Disney).

Below: Extra Jack and Charlie Shirley Beavan lead eventual winner Geordies Express and Kevin Anderson during the Men's Open race at Alnwick.

A huge crowd at Dunthrop see Aztec Rule and Scott Joynes lead the Intermediate race with Chaucers Miller (David Turner), left, and Carew Lad (Dai Jones), right. Eventual winner Rodney Trotter (Harry Dowty, yellow cap) is just off the pace.

Above: Bright Approach and Julian Pritchard lead Running Times (James Jenkins) to win the Men's Open race run over four miles at Dunthrop for the Lord Ashton of Hyde's Challenge Cup.

Above: Owner John Burbidge receives the Challenge Cup from Ros Humphries of sponsors Arterial Moving Ltd after the victory of Bright Approach.

Left: Ashley Farrant gathers his thoughts while Lord Atterbury looks pleased with himself before winning the Men's Open race at Barbury Castle.

Above: Heather Irving leads the lady riders into the parade ring for the Hayman-Joyce Ladies' Open race at Dunthrop.

Below: Harry Dowty drives Rodney Trotter, right, to the line for a narrow win in the Intermediate race with Camden Carrig (Nicholas Phillips) second and Esendi (Liam Payter) third at Dunthrop.

Above: Prah Sands puts in a huge leap for Laura Young with Alaska and Wendy Southcombe next to jump during the Ladies' Open race at Larkhill.

Below: Spanish Dolphin wins a Maiden race at Larkhill at the second time of asking for champion lady rider Polly Gundry.

Above: Hallrule gives trainer and ex-jockey David Parker, left, his first winner in the Maiden race at Aln-wick. Also pictured are Verity Green and Lesley Walby, left, rider Pauline Robson and Dominic Green, right.

Above: Court Adjourn and Stuart Morris lead the Maiden race division two at Larkhill followed by Saffron Hill (Fred Hutsby), left, Lord Ken (Nick Phillips, white cap) and The Luddite (Harry Dowty), right.

Below: Norma Shearing, left, Rosemary Treblecox, centre and Erycka Divers, right, with race-cards and a smile on a cold, wet and windy day at Larkhill.

Above: Claire Trim on the scales at Larkhill as Erica Bridge waits to weigh out.

23

BAY Island returns to the unsaddling enclosure unaccompanied after landing a quality open at Weston Park. Rider Adam Wadlow's explanation is that all the connections have passed out with surprise.

Poacher-turned-gamekeeper Andrew Dalton, 1998 men's joint-champion, stands no nonsense from his former changing tent colleagues in his new role as starter, refusing to let them get a flyer.

Guignol Du Cochet triumphs at Thorpe, but a richer prize awaits Steve Flook at the end of the season, his charge taking top spot in the lucrative Brightwells' Challenge.

Lucy Normile's charm - "When she smiled at me, I said I'd buy it," confesses Ray York - persuaded the Surrey handler to part with an exorbitant, by his standards, 2,800gns for Charango Star, but he recoups £90 when the six-year-old goes in at Higham.

Overnight gales demolish the tents at the Suffolk track, but the organisers are quick to arrange for horseboxes to be used as changing rooms.

Paul Sheldrake and Evan Williams both double up as the Welsh season gets under way at Erw Lon, where Fiona Wilson, absent throughout 2003 after snapping her achilles tendon, scores the first of the nine successes which will make her the area's champion lady.

Balisteros, in his final season, makes it win number 31 at Duncombe Park, where he remains unbeaten.

Ashley Farrant takes a clear lead in the championship after a four-timer at Great Trethew, where Michael Miller rides his 100th point-to-point winner. The meeting also sees a change of fortune for Sue Young. Having lost all her belongings in a fire at her mobile home, Sue wears borrowed boots and breeches for her victory on Fossy Bear.

The veteran 60-and-a-bit George Cooper, possibly the country's most senior rider, records a double at Marks Tey, where a rousing reception greets Zoe Turner's success on Celtic Duke, the first triumph for the yard since the untimely death of her father David in December.

Seven meetings are lost to the weather on the final weekend of the month, while those that remain enjoy varying degrees of support. Despite a 12-race card at Bishops Court, some horses still have to be ballotted out, but at Larkhill, just 21 runners go to post.

february

Above: Torrential rain at Chipley Park where Jockey Club spokesperson John Maxse hesitates before taking the plunge.

Right: Front runner Unlimited Free, ridden by owner Dido Harding, leads Coole'sabbot (Mark Walters) to win the PPORA Members' race at Chipley Park.

Above: Maiden race winner Hug The Bend and Darren Edwards, left, take the second last fence with A Romp Too Far (Robbie McCarthy) and Cargo Flight (Ashley Farrant), far side, as the weather worsens at Chipley Park.

Darren Edwards

Right: Martin Atkinson heads
for the relative comforts of the
changing room after winning
division three of the Maiden race
at Chipley Park in Somerset.

Robbie McCarthy

Chris Leigh, race
commentator

Anna De Lisle
Wells

Jack O'Rourke

Above: Intermediate race winner The Kings Fling and Polly Gundry race with Mensch
(Evan Williams), far side, at Chipley Park.

Below: Alpenstock (David Turner), left, jumps with Mister Swallow (Michael Miller)
during the Restricted race at Chipley Park with eventual winner Little Native (Polly
Gundry, grey colours) almost last.

Above: Storm clouds over Larkhill on Salisbury Plain.

Below: Anna De Lisle Wells was soon on her feet after being unseated from Ballyalbert at the last fence of the Restricted race at Larkhill.

Above: Chaucers Miller makes a mistake under David Turner during the Intermediate race at Larkhill.

Left: Needle and thread required at Larkhill.

Above: Lynda Appleby presents owner Ray Geddes and rider Nick Williams with the EDS Coronation Cup after Tales Of Bounty won at Larkhill.

Right: Richard Wilson, clerk of the course at Higham, surveys the remains of the changing tent - demolished by overnight gales.

Right: Didy Rowell, left, Alex Embiricos and Zoe Turner, right, follow Jane Williams into the parade ring at Higham for the Ladies' Open race.

Right: Mozielaw and Morag Neill, centre, jumps with Native Alibi (Charlie Shirley Beavan), left, and Sporty Spice (Laura Hislop) to win the Members' race at Friars Haugh.

Above: Step In Line, ridden by Samantha Hodge, leads Celtic Duke (Zoe Turner), far side, and Paradisio (Amy Stennett) along the back straight at Higham.

Right: Talented rider Andrew Braithwaite was sidelined for several weeks with a shoulder injury after his mount No Penalty fell in a division of the Maiden race.

Below: Last event on the nine-race card at Higham run in fading light. Eventual winner Cantarinho and David Kemp (green and blue check) is up with the pace.

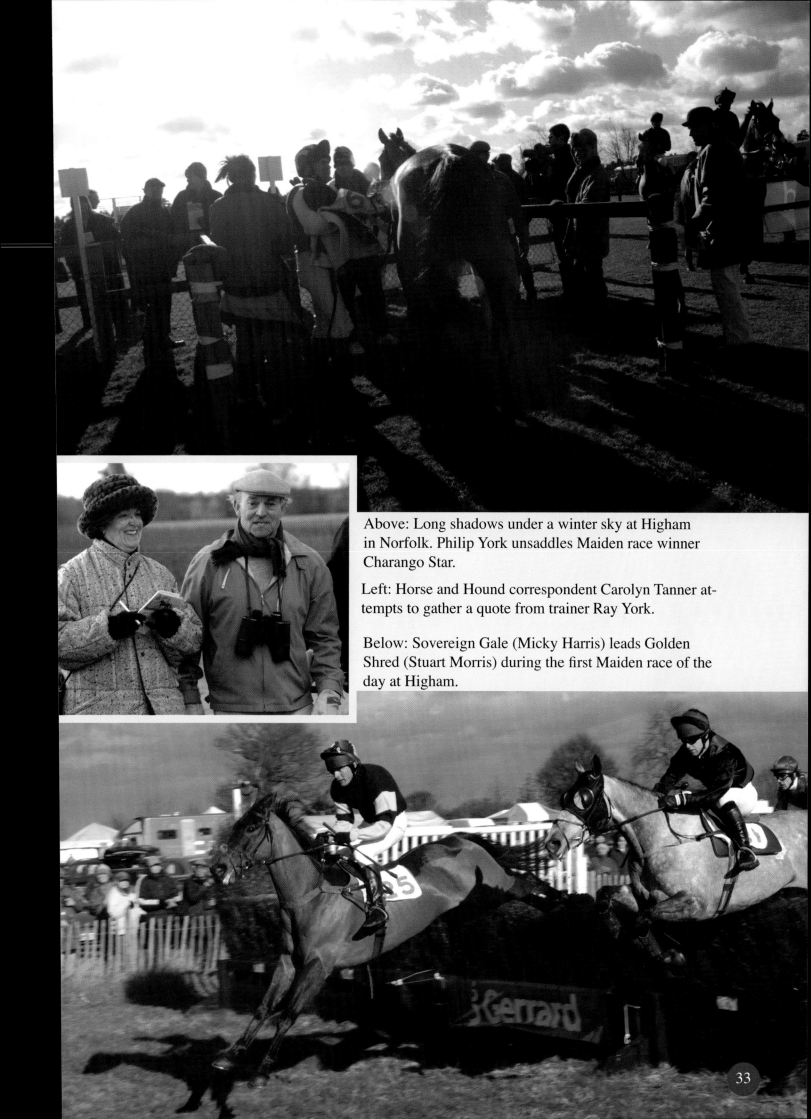

Above: Long shadows under a winter sky at Higham in Norfolk. Philip York unsaddles Maiden race winner Charango Star.

Left: Horse and Hound correspondent Carolyn Tanner attempts to gather a quote from trainer Ray York.

Below: Sovereign Gale (Micky Harris) leads Golden Shred (Stuart Morris) during the first Maiden race of the day at Higham.

Richard Hunnisett

David Kemp

Anthony Williams

Louise Allan

Above: Rheanna Lobley about to part company with Perfect Finisher as Killerine and Heather Irving head for victory in the Kerr-McGee Ladies' Open race at Kingston Blount.

Right: I do! By proposing to Christine Hyde over the PA system on St Valentine's Day at Kingston Blount Tony Cox hits the jackpot by not only securing life membership to the race-course but gaining a new wife.

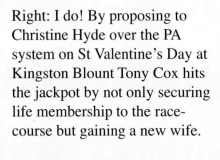

Below: First picnic of the year spotted on St Valentine's Day at Kingston Blount.

Above: Milamoss (Rhys Hughes, red cap), Romany Pearl (James Owen) and Kingfisher Star (Jessie Lodge) chase the leaders during the Waterworld Restricted race at Kingston Blount.

Below: Andy Martin and Cash 'N Carrots fall during the Confined race. Nousayri (20) and Jon Trice Rolph press on at Kingston Blount.

Guy Disney

Susie Tarry

David Phillips, secretary at Milborne St Andrew

Tom Weston

Above: Gangster and Susie Tarry fall as Wild Blade (Rhys Jenkins), left, Dons Delight (Gregor Kerr) and Gunner Sid (Adam Wadlow), right, gallop down the back straight during the Members race at Kingston Blount.

Right: Owner John Phillips and rider George Phillips receive the prizes from Nicola Quesnel after Dinsey Finnegan won the Confined race at Kingston Blount.

Below: Young racegoer at Kingston Blount comes to face with Men's Open winner Father Andy.

Above: Rustic Revelry (Charles Whittaker), left, and Kingston Banker (Harry Wallace) land running as Pearl Dante (Tim Hampton, green colours) hampers Mouseski (Harry Fry) during the CA Members' race for novice riders.

Below: Milborne St Andrew in Dorset where riders make their way through the huge Sunday afternoon crowd.

Above: The Members' race field passes the judge for the first time at a packed Milborne St Andrew where Druid's Brook (Kirsty Reynolds) just leads on the inside.

Below: Racegoers collect free bales of hay at Milborne St Andrew which were generously donated by Langham Farms.

Above: Sally Godfrey greeted by her son Ben (3) and daughter Emma (5) after her Confined Maiden ride on Romany Move at Milborne St Andrew.

Above: Local businessman Jimmy Pike, far right, presents the silverware to rider Martin Atkinson and supporters after Cherokee Boy's popular victory in the CA Members' race for novice riders at Milborne St Andrew.

Below: James Victor (Nick Mitchell) and Young Lirrup (Richard Woollacott) jump ahead of Romany Move (Sally Godfrey) during the Confined Maiden race at Milborne St Andrew.

Above: Miss O'Grady at Milborne St Andrew with rider Michael Miller, lass Sam Johnson, and owner Jill Miller after winning the Westover Land Rover Men's Open race.

Sam Beddoes

Tom Phillips

David England

Walter Puddifer

Above: Rightun and Thomas Ellis lead Igloux Royal (Michael Smith) past the judge with a circuit to go to win the Maiden race division one at Mollington.

Left: Jane Thornton and Richard Burton receive the Lord Bicester Gold Cup from John O'Neill of sponsors Clancy.

Below: Ian Howe leads the Maiden race on Lady Baronette with Vivaldi Rose (Neil Walker), far side, and Polly Flinders (Stuart Morris) at Mollington.

Above: Mollington Men's Open race front-runners Contingency (Rowan Cope), left, Watchyourback (Sam Gray) and Crown And Cushion (James Owen), right, jump the second fence.

Below: Paddy For Paddy (Richard Burton) takes the last fence with Freedom Fighter (Andy Martin), far side, to win the Men's Open sposored by Clancy at Mollington.

David Greenaway

Harriet Gosling,
secretary at
Mollington

Tracey Habgood

Emily Jones

Above: Ladies' race contestants return to the Mollington unsaddling enclosure with Tracey Habgood and Polo Pony bringing up the rear.

Below: Confined race runners Jonno (Tim Lane) and Kupto (Paul Cowley), far side, at the top of the hill at Mollington.

Above: Riders come under Starter's Orders for the last race on Mollington's nine-race card.

Below: Paul Cowley and Shortcut Shorty, far side, pass Andrew Barlow and Et Light in the last strides to win the Members' race at Mollington.

Rosemary Gasson

ROSEMARY Gasson trains a handful of horses near picturesque Balscote in Oxfordshire on a 250-acre property share-farmed with her son Nick. It soon becomes apparent to the visitor that good housekeeping is thoroughly observed on the Gasson patch from the neatly mowed grass to the spotless stables and the freshly harrowed gallops. Her unorthodox training methods have resulted in numerous winners with the victory of Romany Chat, who landed a Cheltenham hunterchase ridden by Andy Martin in 2001, being one of the highlights. Rosemary houses her string together in an open barn where despite the 'occasional snapping' the horses all get along well in their spacious surroundings. Apart from the regular rations from national and local suppliers Rosemary allows the horses a 'huge amount' of carrots daily 'especially in the mornings'. The horses in training

Freedom Fighter and
Andy Martin in action
at Dingley.

are worked every day on the steep hillside gallops
while the youngsters are loose-schooled over logs
and tyres in the yard where they soon become
nimble-footed. Relentless traffic to and from the
local 'top-of-the-tables' primary school has forced
the horses off the roads completely, so all walking is
done in the covered horse-walker. As far as the
current point-to-point situation goes Rosemary
would like to see the season start in October as

it does in Ireland. She thinks 2m and 2m4f races
should be held for pointers who barely get the
regular three miles though probably not to be
ridden by novices and, not surprisingly, allowing
professional trainers to run horses in hunterchases
does not go down well in the Gasson corner of
Oxfordshire!

Above: Richard Darke comes under the torchlight of Clerk of the Scales Valentine Tresidder after winning the Confined race on Ronans Choice at Ottery St Mary.

Right: Ottery St Mary supremo Oliver Carter, right, greets 1960s' winning rider Sarah Rising on the course.

Below: Polly Gundry leads the Ladies' Open race on Sailors Folly with Major Belle (Lucy Bridges), left, and Sadler's Realm (Lucy Gardener) at Ottery St Mary.

Tabitha Cave after Early River collided with a wing during the Open Maiden race at Ottery St Mary.

Mary Finch

Alison Tory

Nick McDiarmind

Freddie De Giles

Above: Fading light at Ottery St Mary where Lord Anner (Nick Williams), far side, races with Lady Blackthorn (Nick McDiarmind) during the Open Maiden race.

Right: Lee Tibbatts, right, back racing at Ottery St Mary after his career as a professional jockey was cut short through injury.

Below: Ollie Jackson takes a crashing fall as the tiring River Dante fails to clear the last obstacle of the Restricted race at Ottery St Mary.

Above: The grey Caspers Case (Nick Williams) and Sir D'Orton (Charlotte Tizzard) cornering well during the Confined race at Ottery St Mary.

Left: Veteran course commentator Alfie Sherrin - brother of radio and TV personality Ned - relays the action at Ottery St Mary in Devon.

Below: By My Side (Alex Charles Jones). right, leads the Intermediate field at Ottery St Mary with Simply Sam (Nick Williams, red cap) and Soul King (Ryan Bliss), left, just off the pace.

Ottery St Mary in Devon.

2003/04 GRADE 1 WINNING IRISH POINT-TO-POINT GRADUATES

BEEF OR SALMON (IRE)
John Durkan Memorial Punchestown Chase (Gr.1)
Punchestown Heineken Gold Cup (Gr.1)

BEST MATE (IRE)
Cheltenham Gold Cup (Gr.1)
Ericcson Chase (Gr.1)

FLORDIA PEARL (IRE)
Hennessy Cognac Gold Cup (Gr.1)

FUNDAMENTALIST (IRE)
Royal & SunAlliance Novices' Hurdle (Gr.1)

STRONG FLOW (IRE)
Feltham Novices' Chase (Gr.1)
Hennessy Cognac Gold Cup (Gr.3)

HI CLOY (IRE)
Powers Gold Cup (Gr.1)

OTHER PRINCIPLE WINNERS INCLUDE:

BINDAREE (IRE)
Coral Welsh National (Gr.3)

FORK LIGHTNING (IRE)
William Hill National Hunt Handicap Chase (Gr.3)

BALLYBOUGH RASHER (IRE)
Charlie Hall Chase (Gr.2)

INEXORABLE (IRE)
Dorans Pride Novice Hurdle (Gr.3)
Cork Stayers Novice Hurdle (Gr.3)

OUR VIC (IRE)
Reynoldstown Novices' Chase (Gr.2)

KEEN LEADER (IRE)
Tommy Whittle Chase (Gr.2)

TAKAGI (IRE)
Bobbyjo Chase (Gr.3)

THEREALBANDIT (IRE)
Lombard Properties Handicap Hurdle (LR)

For information on point-to-points and bloodstock sales in Ireland including details of our Flight/Ferry Reimbursement Scheme for overseas purchasers call + 353-45-443060.

IRISH THOROUGHBRED MARKETING
www.itm.ie

The Curragh, Co. Kildare, Ireland.
Tel: +353-45-443 060 Fax: +353-45-443 061
E-Mail: info@itm.ie

Above: Philip York puts Eastern Point into overdrive to pass Nomadic Star (Zoe Lilley) on the run-in and land the Confined race at Larkhill.

Below: Teller Of Tales and Victoria Flood take the ditch in their stride to land the CA Club Members' race at Larkhill.

Above: Victoria's Boy and Guy Brewer, left, jump with Extra Jack (Charlie Shirley Beavan) to win the Mens' Open race at Hornby Castle in Yorkshire.

Above: Rider Annabel Turner and her mother Anna with New Ross, winner of the four-mile Larkhill National Mixed Open race.

Below: Nariar gives Adam Draycott a heavy fall at the last fence of the Members' race at Larkhill.

TWO trebles on the first weekend give Richard Burton a share of the championship lead with Phil York and Ashley Farrant, but the latter equals the six winner haul a week later, including his second four-timer of the season.

Former lady champion Alison Dare, who made her debut and also rode her initial winner at Didmarton, achieves her first training success on the same track when legging up Andrew Morley to score on Machalini.

Girl power reigns supreme at Charlton Horethorne, where every placing (apart from those in the men's open, not surprisingly) is filled by female riders.

Sixteen-year-old Algan, hero of Kempton's 1994 King George VI chase, returns from a four-year racecourse absence to land the confined at Horseheath.

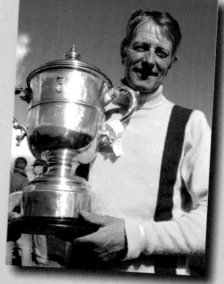

The new course at Brafield-on-the-Green receives the thumbs-up from riders, including Fred Hutsby, the only jockey to hit the deck on the day, and clerk of the course Graeme Tawell, right.

Stephen Swiers, one of very few amateurs to record a century both between the flags and under Rules, announces his retirement, and popular Welsh rider Steve Blackwell also hangs up his boots.

Paul Chinery, at 44 one of the more mature novice riders, already has the lead, never to be relinquished, in the Harley Racing/PPORA points series.

Nick Williams and Richard Barber combine for a treble at Buckfastleigh, where Sandy Duff gives Mary McCarthy the first of the victories which will see her crowned national novice champion.

The colours carried to success by Martin Benson's Windsor Lad in the 1934 St Leger appear in the winner's enclosure in slightly less exalted circumstances after Ed Walker takes the Larkhill Maiden on View Hollo, owned by Martin's granddaughter Jane Arnold.

Gale-force winds bring about the abandonment of the VWH and Holcombe, while the Hurworth is forced to call a halt after four races when conditons play havoc with the fence wings. The following day, six obstacles have to be omitted in one race at Mollington, the problem being low sun.

David Pipe, who bet his mother Carol and Pam Deal £100 that Ballysicyos would have won six races by the end of the campaign, saddles the gelding to land the first of them at Kilworthy. Unfortunately for David, his charge fails by one to meet the target.

march

Below: Owner Peter Clarke with the Duchess of Beaufort and Karen Richards, right, of sponsors Plantagenet Energy Ltd after the victory of Friar Waddon in the Mixed Open race at Didmarton.

Above: Pulham Downe and Emma Tory in the Didmarton parade ring before the Intermediate race.

Below: Maiden race winner Brass Razoo and Stuart Morris lead with a circuit to go at Didmarton. Final Magic (Alex Charles Jones, 20) and Beau Jake (Richard Armson, blue) give chase.

Above: Intermediate race winner Skip 'N' Tune and Michael Miller, left, jump the last fence with Kerstino Two and Jamie Snowden at Didmarton.

Right: Top Welsh rider Tim Vaughan moves on to nearby Charlton Horethorne after finishing unplaced on Itsallupintheair in the second race at Didmarton.

Below: Michael Keel guards his lunch in the changing tent at Didmarton.

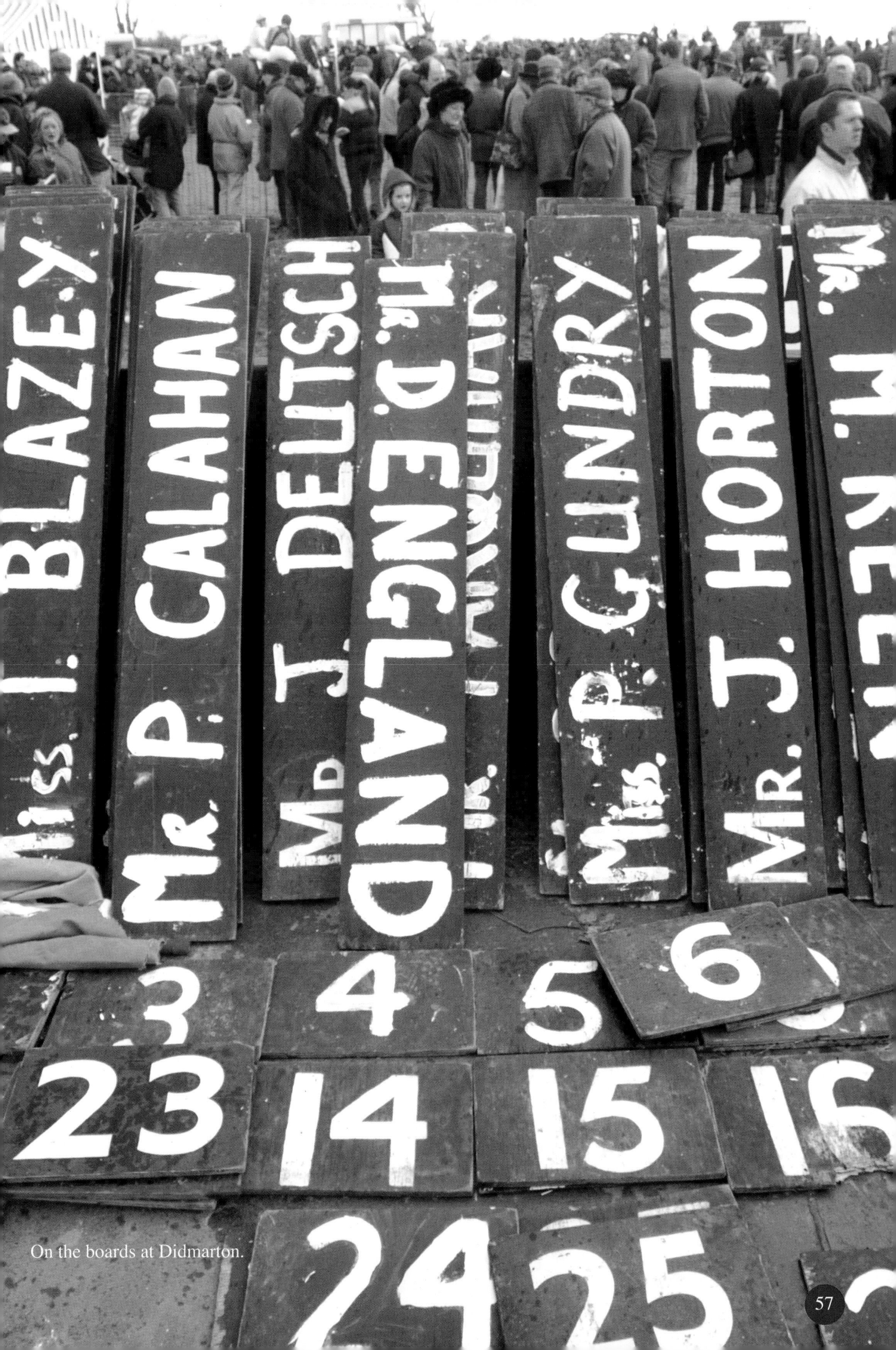

On the boards at Didmarton.

MISS I. BLAZEY
MR P. CALAHAN
MR T. DEUTSCH
MR D. ENGLAND
MR P. GUNDRY
MR J. HORTON
MR M.

3   4   5   6

23   14   15   16

24   25

Above: Silk St Bridget (Gerrard Tumelty), left, jumps with Ham Lane (Fred Hutsby) during the Open Maiden race at Didmarton.

Right: Natalie Lloyd and Star Changes, winners of the Intermediate race for novice riders at Garnons.

Below: New trainer Alison Dare, left, rider Andrew Morley and lass Lois Chappel with Machalini after winning the Members' race at Didmarton.

Above and below: Maiden race runners arrive at the 2m4f miles start at Charing. Siobhans Quinner (David Phelan), left, Sloe Coach (Gareth Wigley, Almazard (Peter Bull), Naughty Noah (Gordon Gallagher) and Toujours (Chris Gordon), right. Below: The first fence causes a few problems as Phil York sets the pace on Royal Cruise.

Left: Secretary Sue Addington Smith with Clerk of the Course Alexander Ball.

Above: Struggles Glory and Stuart Robinson lead Satchmo (Philip Hall), left, Espirit De Cotte (Philip York) and Good Heart (Peter Bull), right, during the Land Rover Men's Open race at Charing.

Left: Mark Nicholas of Barretts Land Rover, right, presents the trophies to Gavin Wragg, Di Grissell and rider Peter Bull after Satchmo won at Charing.

Below: Meander and Jeremy MacTaggart win the Confined race at Corbridge in Northumberland.

Above: Indian Wings (William Hill), left, and Dancing Fosenby (Michael Holdforth) lead the Members' field at a rainswept Charing in Kent. Eventual winner Tell The Nipper and Marcus Gorman (yellow colours) in rear.

Below: Arctic Penguin (Philip York) leads eventual winner Rainbow Ranch (Chris Gordon) and Battle Honours (Philip Hall) during the Restricted race at Charing.

Brightwells Ascot sales: "A great place to find reasonably-priced horses with or without form" - Chris Lawson, point-to-point rider and trainer.

You've bought your next winner with Brightwells Auctioneers, now insure it with Brightwells Insurance.

Leading the field in Sales and Insurance

Brightwells

For all enquiries:

Sales: 01568 619777
Insurance: 01568 619719
www.brightwells.com

Andrew Hanly

Richard Burton

Tino Mastoras

Jon Trice Rolph

Above: Tim Underwood unseats from Madmariea during the restricted race at Charing.

Right: National Hunt legend Bobby Beasley on duty at Charing judging 'best turned out'

Below: The Sky Is Blue and Philip York lead Master Chief (Peter Bull) at the second last to win the Maiden race at Charing.

Above: Clerk of the Course Graeme Tawell in full flow on Bold Statement during the Members' race at the new venue of Brafield on the Green in Northamptonshire.

Below: The spacious parade ring at Brafield on the Green where Maiden race connections await the bell.

Above: The grey General Confusion (Barbara Czepulkowski) lead the Ladies' Open race field at Brafield on the Green followed by Gortroe Guy (Kate Robinson.)

Below: Killerine and Heather Irving win the Briggs & Forrester Ladies' Open race at Brafield on the Green.

Below: Hon secretary at Brafield on the Green Liz Mitchinson with clerk of the scales Ron Duncan.

Above: A heavy shower sweeps across the course at Brafield on the Green as Rightun unseats Thomas Ellis during the Dodson & Horrell PPORA Members' race. Greet You Well (Rowan Cope), far side, leads.

Right: Medical officers Tim Vaughan Lane, left, and Peter Sewell on duty at Brafield on the Green.

Below: The parade ring at Whitwick Manor, near Hereford.

Above: Maiden race winner Born To Dream (Rowan Cope), centre, races with Sandyland (Andrew Sansome), left, and Native Thunder (Sally Duckett), right at Brafield on the Green.

Right: Brafield declarations' operatives Dale Dickins, left, Val Good, centre, and Maire Duncan.

Below: Ballysicyos unseats Ollie Jackson at the first fence of the Ladies' Open race at Cothelstone.

Above: Men's Open race winner Speed Board and Jason Cook, far side, jump with Lyphard's Fable (David England) and the grey Persona Pride (Jon Trice Rolph) at Whitwick Manor.

Left: Steve Hughes and Legend Of Light look to have the measure of Snitton West (Mark Jackson) at the last only to become unseated on the run-in of the Maiden race at Whitwick Manor.

Above: Dai Jones takes a crashing fall after Crystal Soldier comes to grief during the Confined Maiden race at Llanfrynach.

Right: Anna Blake is consoled after being unseated from Dunston Heath in the Ladies' race at Whitwick Manor.

Below: Ears pricked, the grey Persona Pride and Julian Pritchard dispute the early lead in the Confined race at Brampton Bryan in Herefordshire.

Above: Men's Open winner Imps Way (Lee Bates, red) amongst the leaders with a circuit to run at Hutton Rudby.

Left: The beer tent suffers as wild weather sweeps across the course at Hutton Rudby in Yorkshire.

Below: James Owen drives Finder Keeps to the line to defeat Stennikov(Ed Walker), right, and Sing High (Andy Martin), left, on the run-in for the Intermediate race at Mollington.

Guy Weatherley

Robert Hodges

Rachel Reynolds

Ray Rogers

Above: Wild Blade and Rhys Jenkins have lift-off at the ditch during the Confined race at Whitwick Manor.

Right: Winning owners Deborah and Dennis Pugh with rider Jason Cook, lad Steve Rooney and Whitwick Manor Men's Open winner Speed Board.

Below: Caught At Dawn puts in a fine leap for Tom Weston to win the Denco Confined race at Whitwick Manor.

WISH LIST FOR 2005 by Carolyn Tanner

That organisers can somehow manage to reach a compromise over their fixture dates. The ridiculous Larkhill-Tweseldown clash in 2004 at the start of the season did no favours to anybody. Different days would have given competitors more options, and both meetings would have seen increased gates. Sadly, no lessons have been learned, and the same situation will arise in 2005. Clashes such as this, in adjacent areas, are bad enough, but those who hold two fixtures within their own area on the same day need their heads knocking together, while four meetings in the space of as many days in the North West area has always been a ludicrous situation.

That there will be no ballotting out. With just a modicum of common sense, this could have been avoided at both fixtures at which daylight ran out in 2004. One, which had a massive entry and was almost certain to attract huge declarations, should have brought forward the start time, and the other needed only to adjust the race times on the day, which could have been easily done.

Point-to-point organisers give their time voluntarily, for which competitors are often too slow to express their gratitude, but they need to remember that it is the owners and trainers who supply the sport which helps to make money for the hunt. A lot of time, effort and expense has been put into getting a horse to a meeting, so to have to return home without a run, when it is not of their choosing, is little short of a disgrace.

That those hunts which have very few subscribers will amalgamate their hunt race with one of their neighbours. This is already done successfully by some, who continue to present their own trophies. Let us not forget that point-to-pointing is a leisure industry which needs to attract paying customers, who will not appreciate being short-changed by having to watch a two horse race, or at worst, a walkover.

That late season meetings will not divide races before the day, however many entries they get. How many times do we see less than half a dozen runners in each division of a maiden, due to the ground firming up?

That judges will not wait for an age before announcing the result of a close finish. There are no photo finish cameras in point-to-pointing, so why a long delay?

That commentators will not have to stand out in the open to perform their task. There is no excuse for not providing some shelter, even if it is just a tarpaulin draped on some scaffolding.

That sponsors will receive the treatment they deserve. Full marks to the Hurworth, who provide a marquee for their use, and also arrange for some of the jockeys to preview the day's racing.

That, for the benefit of lady riders, there are fewer mixed open races. It is an oft heard plea from the girls, who are at a disadvantage in these contests due to having to carry more lead.

That, and this is the most fervent wish of all, every horse and rider returns home safely.

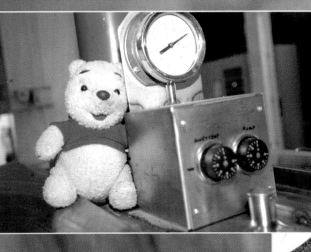

FEEDING horses properly is a complicated business as anyone visiting the Baileys Mill and preparation plant near Braintree, Essex, will discover. A massive building full of mysterious machinery and delicious cooking smells operates 24 hours a day from Monday to Friday to produce feeds needed "for everything from fluffy Shetlands to Guineas winners". Baileys know all about Guineas winners as they had their very own classic hero in Mister Baileys. Managing director Paul Venner breeds bloodstock and bought Mister Baileys as a foal who went on to win the 2,000 Guineas in 1994. The bakery smells come from the fearsome-looking

Micronser machines which transform natural ingredients into something that looks and smells like toasted muesli. "We cook everything we can to make it more digestible," said Mark Buchan, sales manager and point-to-point enthusiast. Ingredients for the 30 lines that are produced and bagged at the plant range from bulk crops stored in huge silos down to bags of specialist ingredients which are added by hand to the final mix. A recent addition is the huge vat of warm honey swirled about by mechanical paddles and watched over by an eagle-eyed teddy bear! "Grain trader Mike Sheppard of North Herts Farmers buys on our behalf and we

use our own trucks to collect bulk from mostly local farms. Liquid products like molasses and soya oil are delivered by tankers," explains Mark. "We use non-GM ingredients and often have to pay a premium to ensure their traceability." The Ministry of Agriculture makes monthly visits to take samples and before any feeds leave the mill samples from each batch are collected, labelled and stored in glass containers for analysis to detect any prohibited substances. When it comes to feeding horses nothing is left to chance. Since they began trading 22 years ago Baileys Horse Feeds have, in racing terms, made rapid progress and are up with the leaders in their field. What's the secret? The answer is a combination of nutritional expertise and knowledge of the horse world which has developed since Venner and sales director George Knowles founded the company with the idea that they could fill a gap in the market by providing the first 'non-heating' feed. That product was Baileys Number One Cooked Cereal Meal, based on the bread that was already passing through the plant. Gradually the feed business took over and has branched out and flourished to such an extent that the equine fraternity have been happily dining on their products ever since.

Christie's Foxhunter Steeple Chase at Cheltenham.

Left: Woodlands Beau (Tom Dreaper) is followed in the parade ring by Upham Lord (Guy Brewer) and Lord Atterbury.

Above: Riders Nick Mitchell, right, and Tom Dreaper test the Cheltenham going before racing.

Below: Heavy rain greets the riders as they leave the changing room. Nick Mitchell is followed by Alex Charles Jones and Dale Jewett

Below: The field reach the first fence where Geordies Express unseats Dale Jewett. Front runners are Polar Champ (Tom Malone, red), Bosuns Mate (Belinda Keighley), Sheriff's Friend (Chris Gordon, yellow sleeves) and Spot Thedifference (John McNamara, green).

Above: A circuit to run and Polar Champ (Tom Malone) leads Bosuns Mate (Belinda Keighley), Irbee (Charlotte Tizzard, red) with Lord Atterbury (Ashley Farrant, green sleeves) handily placed. Eventual winner Earthmover (yellow, extreme left) is biding his time.

Left: As the Irish roar rolls down from the grandstand for Never Compromise and Derek O'Connor, left, Dorset's Rilly Goschen asks the 13-year-old Earthmover for a final effort to land the season's biggest prize.

Right: Rilly Goschen and the impressive Christie's Challenge Cup are the focus of attention as Royal photographer Bernard Parkin (green jacket, flat cap) and common snappers get their pictures.

Noel Wilson

Kayley Jones

Anthony Ward
Thomas

Helen Gordon

Above: Merry Shot puts in a huge leap for Jamie Snowden during the Men's Open race at Badbury Rings.

Right: Matt Hardy, left, of sponsors Wyles Hardy presents trophies to owner James Drummond and rider Dominic Alers Hankey after Out The Black won the Men's Open race at Badbury Rings.

Below: Officials survey the remains of the ladies' changing tent at Friars Haugh after fierce storms swept across the entire British Isles overnight.

Above: Thunder Thighs and Nathan Wilmington, left, pass Hawkers Hill (Nick Mitchell) at the second last to land the Restricted race at Badbury Rings.

Left: Owners Nick Freak and Chris Kendall and rider Nathan Wilmington receive their spoils from meeting secretary Catherine Elgar at Badbury Rings.

Below: Little Mister and Nick Mitchell, left, race with Pandeli (David Phelan) during the Maiden race at Badbury Rings in Dorset.

Above: The Cooling Agent (Michael Miller), My Little Lady (Amanda Bush) and The Nelson Touch (David Turner) follow eventual winner Lord Alpha (David Phelan) during the Maiden race at Badbury Rings.

Below: Sherbourne Guest (Jan Kwiatkowski), right, jumps with Coolteen Hero (Daryl Jacob) and eventual winner Simply Sam (Harry Fry) during the CA Members' race for novice riders at Badbury Rings.

Above: Wind problems at Badbury Rings.

Above: A full house lines the uphill finish at Godstone in Surrey.

Left: Natalie Moisey and Castle Arrow lead the Ladies' Open race contestants in the parade ring at Godstone.

Right: James Sarchet follows Paul Chinery (blue/white quarters), Andrew Coveney (sash) and Jeremy Wall (purple) into the Godstone ring for the CA Members' race for veteran and novice riders.

81

Wayne Kavenaugh

Gordon Gallagher

Harry Fry

Jeremy Wall

Above: Quick Response and Brea Donnelly in full flow during the Confined race at Godstone.

Left: Tom Cobbler and Pippa Hall take the last fence to win the Highfields Farm Ladies' Open race at Godstone.

Below: George Cooper holds a temporary lead in the Godstone Confined race on Jims Belief with Garrison Friendly (Noel Wilson, green) and eventual winner Lively Lord (Chris Gordon) just off the pace.

Above: Veterans and novice riders unsaddle at picturesque Godstone.

Left: Stuart Robinson with his father David after Struggles Glory won the Men's Open race sponsored by Kent Commercials at Godstone.

Below: Paul Chinery explains the outcome of the veterans' and novices' race to a youngster in the Godstone changing tent.

Above: Toujours and Chris Gordon win the Restricted race at Godstone.

Right: Nigel Wilson, meeting secretary at Godstone, enjoys a cup of tea after racing.

Below: Getting competitive at Godstone in the Members' race where Chris Gordon on Alice Reigns, right, and eventual winners Philip Hall and Jack Hackett, left, leave Peter Bull on the grey Straight Baron little room to manoeuvre on the run-in.

Above: Novice riders' race winner Boyne Banks (Guy Disney) leads Keegan Bearnais (Tom Mann) and O'Flaherty's (Wayne Kavenaugh) with a circuit to run at Larkhill.

Above: Men's Open race riders at Larkhill are from left, Martin Sweetland, Neil Harris, Bobby McEwen, Nick Williams and Daryl Jacob.

Above: Threads of gold on the wrist of Royal rider Bobby McEwen.

Right: No way back for Rupert Tory as Warren Hill falls at the last fence of the Larkhill Novice Riders' race.

Sarah Lane

Mark Munrowd

Jeremy Mahot

Nick Oliver

Above: The Sycophant and Ryan Bliss skip over the birch with Ring Off and Jack O'Rourke on his heels during the Confined maiden race at Larkhill.

Left: James Gray MP, centre, presents the Ladies' Open trophies to John Snook and Terry Hamlin, left, and Polly Gundry and Martin Dare, right, after What A Mover won at Larkhill.

Below: Polly Gundry steers What A Mover to Ladies' Open race sucess at Larkhill.

Above: Novice riders in action at Ston Easton in Somerset where the grey Aldington Charlie (Charlie Sands) leads Glenahary Rose (Alison Tory), left, Supreme Storm (Richard Bandey, pink sleeves) and Rustic Revelry (Charles Whittaker), right.

Right: Viv Grundy, joint secretary at Maisemore Park, comes under the protection of photographer Chris Cook.

Right: Who said 'never give a horse a bad name'? Marc Barber steers Beasley into second place in the Confined maiden race at Cilwendeg.

Above: A scramble to the line for Maiden race honours at Maisemore Park where Tim Stephenson on Blackanblue, far side, just lose out to Harry Dowty on Lord Ken.

Above: A day to remember for Geoff Barfoot Saunt after Ebony Jack won division two of the Maiden race at Maisemore Park.

Left: A day to forget for former champion Julian Pritchard whose rides at Maisemore Park included a fall, an unseated and a refusal.

Above: The Mixed Open race field stream over the last fence on their first circuit at Maisemore Park.

Right: The Lads and Lasses syndicate line up, from left, Betty Norman, June Green, Tim Holt, Sue Holt and Craig Norman with rider Alex Charles Jones to receive the magnificent Lady Bullough Cup from Martin Dawe, rear, after Polar Flight won at Maisemore Park.

Right: Polar Fight puts in a fine leap at the last for Alex Charles Jones to land the Gerald Dawe Memorial Mixed Open race at Maisemore Park.

RICHARD Burton cuts Ashley Farrant's championship lead to three with a treble at Tabley. The first leg, Indian Wings, gives the jockey his 150th success between the flags. Another three-timer follows on Easter Tuesday at Flagg Moor, which hosts a meeting for the first time since 2000. Freedom Fighter runs his 61st race and wins at Andoversford. He has been ridden on every occasion by Andy Martin. By the end of the season the unbroken partnership has risen to 65 races and ten victories.

Sad Mad Bad and owner Grant Tuer land the Grimthorpe Gold Cup, and a fortnight later, another of the classic races, the Lady Dudley Cup, goes to schoolboy Tom Weston on his father's Caught At Dawn, who at the end of the month goes on to hunterchase success at Cheltenham.

Julian Pritchard, out of action for several weeks with a badly damaged collarbone, gets back on the scoresheet with a Bitterley victory. But the 2003 novice champion Chris Gillon decides against a comeback from injury and bows out of racing altogether.

Trainer David Parker keeps up his remarkable strike rate – eight winners from ten runners to date – but Anna Brooks, with five out of seven when Wincy Spider obliges at Cottenham, is not far behind.

Former conditional Lee Stephens rides his first winner since reverting to amateur status, Cooleen Strong at Ystradowen. Despite leaving it until mid-April to open his account, his tally has reached 11 by the end of the season.

Polly Gundry is the only treble scorer on Easter Monday, when the Phillips brothers, Nick and George, ride a winner apiece at Lockinge, and a trio of jockeys, namely Charlotte Stucley, Ashley Farrant and Nick Williams, land a double apiece at Kingston St Mary.

Down and Sam Waley-Cohen complete a hat-trick of victories in the Welsh Grand National at Bonvilston. Sam receives his bottle of champagne from his old school matron, who points out that her former pupil is still, as ever, in need of a haircut!

Farrier Andy Brown, above, proves that ambitions can be realised at 40 when Crackrattle carries him to victory at Clifton-upon-Dunsmore. Andy is reportedly still celebrating several weeks later.

april

Above: A vast crowd waits expectantly for the action to begin at Badbury Rings in Dorset.

Below: Sweet Kari (Guy Weatherley), left, races with Red Risk (Martin Sweetland) and Tycoon Red (Richard Woollacott), right, during the Restricted race at Cherrybrook.

Above: Local businessman and racing benefactor Jimmy Pike presents the annual terrier race prize to Karen Hughes and Dylan.

David Mansell

Sarah Buckley

Lenny Hicks

Catherine Atkinson

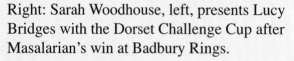

Above: Sad Mad Bad and Grant Tuer lead Erzadjan (Lee Bates) to win the prestigious Grimthorpe Gold Cup at Whitwell on the Hill in Yorkshire.

Right: Sarah Woodhouse, left, presents Lucy Bridges with the Dorset Challenge Cup after Masalarian's win at Badbury Rings.

Below: The impressive Free Gift (Daryl Jacob) glides over the last at Badbury Rings to win the CA Club race for novice riders.

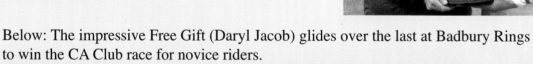

Above: Merry Shot (Jamie Snowden) follows Beadnell Bay (Rilly Goschen) on the first circuit of the Mixed Open race at Badbury Rings.

Right: The parade ring at Badbury Rings.

Below: Inner State (Darren Edwards), left, disputes the lead with Polar Bright (Nick Mitchell) during the Open Maiden race at Kingston St Mary in Somerset.

Above: The hard-pulling Near And Phar (Sarah Buckley) leads Moscow Tradition (Joe Docker, blue) in the Restricted race at Thorpe Lodge. Confusion reigned after Buckley bypassed several fences but went on to

Left: An accident waiting to happen at Thorpe Lodge. With the crowd positioned head-on to the last fence it was only a matter of time. Gemma Hutchinson's mount Silver Buzzard falls leaving Gillone and Joe Docker to win the Mixed Open race.

Below: Scenic Ystradowen where Tim Vaughan on Westar Lad lead the Open Maiden race field.

Above: King's Hero (Stuart Morris, yellow) and Bengal Boy (Nick Pearce) sail over the Thorpe Lodge fences during the Confined race.

Right: Anne Jepson, secretary and treasurer at Thorpe Lodge, and for whom nothing is too much trouble.

Below: Flat to the boards on the final bend at Thorpe Lodge as Runningwiththemoon (Matthew Briggs), right, prevails over Orchestra Boy (Kevin Green) in the Open Maiden race.

Nick Docker

Rachel Reynolds

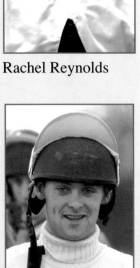

Stuart Morris

Richard Armson

Above: Russian Friend and Richard Collinson take the last fence at Thorpe Lodge to land the Open Maiden race sponsored by Beachill Ltd.

Left: Owner/trainer Mary Samworth, right, with Arthur Rhodes and Brenda Dutton after Russian Friend won at Thorpe Lodge.

Below: The bookmaker line attracts plenty of punters at Thorpe Lodge in Nottinghamshire.

Above: Touchez Du Bois and Tommy Morrison win the Members' race from Valley Garden and French Chocolate at Dalston in Cumbria.

Right: Posh Stick and Jimmy Walton after winning the Maiden race at Dalston.

Michelle Hugo

Richard Collinson

Sue Sharratt

Tim Park

Above: Spectators at Flagg Moor, Derbyshire, for the annual point-to-point races.

Below: Aunt Gladys (Guy Brewer), left, jumps with Ridware Pride (Sue Sharratt) during the PPORA Members' Restricted race at Flagg Moor.

Above: Corporal Sarah Goddard flogging Flagg Moor racecards at the popular Derbyshire Peaks venue.

Right: Narrisa Brady with the High Peak Cup and the Jim Wood Memorial Cup after her sucess on Tellitasitis in the stone wall race.

Below: The stone wall race where Nick Fogg leads on Quinn followed by Fable (Pippa Winn), eventual winner Tellitasitis (Narrisa Brady) and Lily (Dee McKenna).

Above: Jason Burley precedes Richard Burton, Lenny Hicks and Gary Hanmer into the Flagg Moor parade ring.

Right: Hon secretary Sue Rodman making everyone welcome at Flagg Moor.

Below: Class Of Ninetytwo (Sue Sharratt) and Macfin (Louise Allan), far side, lead eventual winner River Ness (Victoria Thirlby) around the picturesque course at Flagg Moor.

Above: Ladies' Open race runners Fami (Gemma Hutchinson), Yer 'Umble (Michelle Hugo), Sea Tarth (Hannah Kinsey) and Supreme Silence (Rachel Clark) at the start watched by the Easter holiday crowd on the rocky hillside at Flagg Moor.

Left: Smiles all round after Blank Cheque and David Coates won the Confined race at Whittington, Lancashire.

Below: Harriet Bethell and Dolphin Square, far side, pass Distracting (Kevin Pearson) to win the Intermediate race at Whittington.

Above: Merry Major (Michael Keel) follows Optimistic Thinker (Andrew Shaw) as the Members' race runners parade at Chaddesley Corbett in Worcestershire.

Left: Fleur Cushman, editor of Racing Post Weekender, presents the prestigious Lady Dudley Cup run at Chaddesley Corbett to Martin Weston, owner of Caught At Dawn.

Below: Tom Weston unsaddles Lady Dudley Cup winner Caught At Dawn at Chaddesley Corbett.

Above: A packed house at Chaddesley Corbett sees the Lady Dudley Cup field stream over the last fence on their first circuit.

Right: Caught At Dawn and Tom Weston take the last fence to land the Lady Dudley Cup sponsored by Racing Post Weekender at Chaddesley Corbett.

Robert Ward Dutton

Kenneth O'Brien

Victoria Thirlby

Oliver Greenall

Above: Sovereign Gale and Micky Harris lead throughout to win the CA Club Members' race for mares at Chaddesley Corbett.

Right: Chaddesley Corbett trade stand operative demonstrating the latest cheekpieces.

Below: Hattie and Philip Cornforth adopt an unorthodox style of riding to win the Maiden race at Corbridge.

Above: Magicien and Rachel Reynolds separate Shaking Chief (Adrian Wintle), left, and Shemardi (Robert Hodges), right, at the last fence to win the Restricted race at Chaddesley Corbett.

Below: Gunners Mistake (Liam Heard), left, Winning Leader (Ollie Jackson), centre, and Cut Down The Sound (Sarah Gaisford), right, race together during the Restricted at Flete Park in Devon.

Dick Baimbridge

MIST swirling over lush green meadows, dark hedgerows and deep irrigation ditches. This is Baimbridge country.

Dick Bainbridge is a countryman through and through. The weatherbeaten face and hands like shovels are testament to years of farming sheep near the banks of the Severn Estuary. Sheep are one thing but horses are Dick's passion in life. He has been around horses for over 60 years, both riding and training. He rode his first winner in 1961 on Jackum at Upton on Severn in the then Coventry Cup. Stable star was Mendip Express who won a remarkable 38 times. Though he won just five races himself in the saddle he has trained around 450 winners between the flags. Both he and his younger brother Harry wanted to ride but their father Harold tossed a coin. Harry called correctly and rode leaving Dick to be appointed chief milker

on the family farm. Champion trainer in the West Midlands on numerous occasions, Dick received a special award for services to point-to-point in 1990 presented at the Belfry national dinner. Travelling horses to other areas as far afield as Cottenham in East Anglia and Badbury Rings near the South Coast was well within his compass when titles were there to be won. Riders like Julian Pritchard and Alison Dare have become champions on the backs of many horses trained on the Baimbridge gallops. Amongst others Geoff Barfoot Saunt, Evan Williams and Adrian Wintle have all benefited from his expertise and more recently Helen Hillard (fomerly Helen Gundry) also rode with success. The biggest name to have flourished from the Baimbridge academy is that of leading National Hunt trainer Paul Nicholls. He started part-time with Dick at the age of 12 and after leaving school at 16 was full-time for about another

Right: Baimbridge trained Father Tom and Julian Pritchard win the Welsh Border Counties Area Confined Hunts Championship Race at Bredwardine.

three years. Nicholls has never forgotten the advice he was given during those formative years: "Dick's attention to detail was second to none and I learned more from him than anyone else. "The horses were fed well and trained hard which resulted in them being supremely fit and disciplined. He could take a mad 12-year-old that had never been sighted and win two or three races with it. "The horses were trained on the very steep hills around his place using the interval method and when I came here (to Ditcheat in Somerset) I knew this was what I wanted – the same kind of steep hill." About the embryonic Nicholls, Dick remembers him as a determined and thick-skinned youngster: "He was a smashing lad and even though I used to call him everything you could never offend him. "I remember once we took two horses to the Leicester hunterchase day. Alison Dare won her race but Paul went flying on his mount

Precipitous. He came back with all the excuses in the world but I said to him 'you fell off him but never mind Paul, it won't happen again because you won't be riding him if that happens many more times'." Alison later rode the horse to win the prestigious John Corbet Cup at Stratford in a photofinish - with Paul leading him up. This year Dick will have around 10 horses in his yard near Dursley in Gloucestershire. Retirement is out of the question with horses already being turned away for the 2005 campaign. A new addition to Dick's workforce this season will be Claire Allen from an adjoining farm and, subject to owners' approval, she will ride the ladies' race horses. "She would certainly ride any of mine," said Dick with enthusiasm which suggests he is looking forward to this season just as eagerly as if it were his first.

107

Raymond James (David Mansell)
leads the Restricted race at Woodford.

Above: Vivid Imagination and Ashley Farrant chase Camden Carrig and Nick Phillips who maintained a relentless gallop to win the Penleys Men's Open race at Woodford.

Below: Phar From Chance and Polly Gundry come home clear to win the Ladies' Open race at Woodford

Above: Thunder Thighs (Nathan Wilmington), left, races Glacial Pearl (Peter Mason), centre, and Stennikov (Ed Walker) for the minor placings in the Intermediate race at Woodford in Gloucestershire.

Above: A busy day for declarations and scales at Woodford.

Below: Ashley Farrant is unseated from Vivid Imagination, left, as Fred Hutsby struggles with Sir Dante during the Men's Open race at Woodford.

Jason Newbold

Rebecca Hutsby

Gerry Moloney

John Maxse

Above: Rosie Booth has no chance as Atavistic gets it wrong two from home leaving eventual winner Let's Fly (William Biddick) clear during the CA Club Members' race for novice riders at Stafford Cross in Devon.

Below: Royalecko and Jane Hollands, right, win the Confined race at Balcormo Mains in Fife.

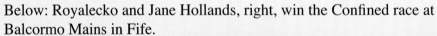

Above: On the turn at Clifton upon Dunsmore where Members' winner Catchphrase and Lenny Hicks lead Shallow River (Hannah Phizacklea) and Strong Chairman (Kenneth O'Brien).

Below: Sunday lunch in the sunshine at Clifton upon Dunsmore.

Above: Riders at Clifton upon Dunsmore in colours that have been worn through generations of jockeys.

Above: Blue Royal (Stuart Morris) and Red Rebel (Rowan Cope), far side, demonstrate the art of jumping during the Men's Open race at Clifton upon Dunsmore.

Below: The parade ring at Clifton upon Dunsmore where the Maiden race runners assemble.

Above: Sarah Garland, hon secretary at Clifton upon Dunsmore, near Rugby.

Above: With victory already out of the question, Paul Newton on Bethin, right, and Paul Cowley on Sams Sister attempt to 'obtain the best possible placing' in the Mares' Open Maiden race at Clifton upon Dunsmore.

Below: Ardmayle (Lucy Coney), far side, jumps with eventual winner Aircon (Rebecca Hutsby) at Clifton upon Dunsmore during the Ladies' race sponsored by James Bennett Ltd.

Above: A day at the races for Debbie Christian and Stephen Nicholls.

Above: The finishing straight at Clifton upon Dunsmore in Warwickshire.

Left: Saint-Declan and rider Stuart Morris after winning division two of the Maiden race at Clifton upon Dunsmore for owners Richard Mathias and Hilary Bubb.

Below: Teeton Glaive (Heather Irving) and Camitrov (Gregor Kerr), far side, lead the Confined race at Clifton upon Dunsmore with Needwood Neptune (Peter Bennett), left.

Above: Sassey's Circle (Nick Pearce), right, and Charlestown Lass (Tim Vaughan) set the pace during the Maiden race for mares at Clifton upon Dunsmore.

Left: Supporters line up with the Harry Barton Challenge Cup after Briery Fox won the Maiden race at Clifton upon Dunsmore.

Below: Maiden race winner Briery Fox (Joe Docker) leads Currow Kate (Lenny Hicks) and Two Oceans (Rowan Cope) with a circuit to race at Clifton upon Dunsmore.

T HE men's championship is a two-horse race, and May begins with Messrs Burton and Farrant both looking certain to beat Julian Pritchard's British record. Ashley is the first one to pass the magic 43, but gives his supporters their customary annual scare by appearing to suffer injury when going through the wing at Trebudannon. Fortunately the blip is temporary. Phil York, who finishes an honourable but distant third in the title race, notches up his century at Aldington.

Three winners early in May take Nicola Stirling's run to seven successes from her last nine rides.

Jenny Gordon, South-East lady champion for the fifth time, retires from the saddle, and Katherine Diggle, a former North West champion, also hangs up her boots.

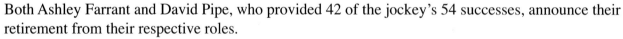

East Anglians take advantage of the £40 travelling expenses paid by the Southdown & Eridge to all runners from out of the area, and win five of the six contests open to them.

Sovereign Gale takes the Panacur/TBA mares' final at Garthorpe for Micky Harris and handler Theresa McCurrich.

Alex Charles-Jones is unlikely to forget Joyful Jade's Trebudannon victory, and not only because it was his 100th success between the flags. Firstly the horses were mistakenly directed to the 2m4f start for this 3m contest, and then Alex rode a finish a circuit too soon before realising his error.

Every winning trainer at Kingston St Mary, where the sun beat down, received an umbrella as a prize. By the end of the evening, David Pipe's tally was four. Three of his winners were partnered by Ashley Farrant, who recorded his 150th on Ballysicyos.

Emma Jones, out of the racing saddle since 1995, wins at Lydstep, where husband Dai rides a double for his father-in-law.

Richard Burton concedes defeat after a blank day at Trecoed. Who would have bet at the start of the season that a jockey would ride 50 winners and not end up as champion? He is present at Umberleigh, though, to shake his successor by the hand, a sporting gesture appreciated by the large crowd.

Both Ashley Farrant and David Pipe, who provided 42 of the jockey's 54 successes, announce their retirement from their respective roles.

Andrew Ayres, left, secretary at Peper Harow, presides over what has been described as point-to-point's 'Regent Street'.

Rilly Goschen's success on Hawkers Hill gives her the runner-up spot in the title race to Polly Gundry.

The barbecues and picnics in the car park continue long into the night as racegoers reminisce about 2004 and start looking forward to 2005.

may/june

Above: Jockey Club spokesman
John Maxse and Gunnerbe Posh
all but demolish the Peper Harow
fence while Phil York stretches
the reins on Royal Cruise during
the Open Maiden race.

Right: Fearless Philip York at Peper Harow after
his Maiden race win on Royal Cruise gained at
the expense of Jockey Club spokesman John
Maxse on Gunnerbe Posh.

Clare Cowe

Dan Dennis

Paul Blagg

Jenny Gordon

Above: The 'Regent Street' of point-to-point racing at Peper Harow in Surrey.

Right: Starter's assistant on duty at Peper Harow.

Below: Chris Gordon and hat-trick seeker Lively Lord enjoy a temporary lead in the Men's Open race at Peper Harow with Dunrig (James Owen) on his heels.

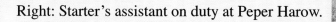

Above: Jamie Snowden and Royal Czarina lead the Restricted race along the causeway to safely negotiate the Peper Harow bog.

Right: On firmer ground, corporate entertainment clients enjoy an elevated view of proceedings at Peper Harow.

Below: Good Heart and Nick Oliver, far side, hold off the challenge of River Bailiff (Philip York) to land the Men's Open race sponsored by BWD Rensburg at Peper Harow .

Chris Lawson

Left: The Lawson trained
Good Thyne Murphy and
Andrew Braithwaite at
Godstone.

IT was June, 2003, when staff at the Financial Times reacted with shock horror to the news that Chris Lawson was leaving after 16 years to pursue a career as a trainer of point-to-pointers. "I think it was a mid-life crisis," says the former City slicker. "Some chaps buy a Harley Davidson, others leave their wife for a teenage dolly-bird. Me? I abandoned a lucrative editorial post on an international newspaper to shovel s**t after other people's horses!" (editor's note: Some may suggest I'd been doing exactly the same for the last 16 years) It was a lifestyle decision and a year on, Chris is supported by a small but loyal band of owners at his yard in Stapleford Tawney, Essex. The proximity of his yard to the M25 is important: "My horses must be the only ones in the country who are schooled on the hard-shoulder of a motorway - it certainly makes them traffic proof! And it means the yard is easy to locate for those who have never been here before." Spectacularly unsuccessful as a jockey over 14 years (though one aberration in 1998 saw him crowned East Anglian champion owner/trainer/rider), he views his penniless future combining training with a freelance journalistic career with an air of nonchalance. "You

get bolshy, difficult horses and you get bolshy difficult editors. After 25 years working in Fleet Street, I know which I prefer!" A word of warning for any prospective owner - to have a horse in the Lawson yard, the possession of a sense of humour is essential. What would he change in pointing given the chance? "I'd want a longer season, just like they do in Ireland - starting in November with a two-three week break over Christmas and New Year, then off again mid-Jan through to the first May Bank Holiday. Firm grounders could have early and late season ground while softer ground types have the middle part of the season. "I'm sure it would mean more runners and better matched races but would also provide better value for potential sponsors to get involved, not just with individual yards/owners/ trainers but with any championship series of races and more meetings to have a corporate presence. "I know this is supposed to be an amateur sport but I think we all realise that to a greater or lesser extent, it no longer is."

Jane Reed

Felix Wheeler

Nigel Benstead

Neil Ransford, Cotley
Farm secretary

Above: Kilvoydan and David Phelan, left, follow Jack Of Kilcash over the ditch during the Confined race at Peper Harow.

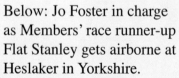

Right: East meets west at Peper Harow. Dorset trainer John Dufosee, right, with East Anglia legend Joe Turner.

Below: Jo Foster in charge as Members' race runner-up Flat Stanley gets airborne at Heslaker in Yorkshire.

Above: Maiden race winner See More Fun and Nick Williams race with Dart View Lass (Nathan Wilmington) at Cotley Farm.

Left: Last-minute instructions for Cotley Farm fence stewards.

Knight Of Passion and Charlotte Tizzard lead Dale Creek (Michael
Miller) to win the Members' race at Cotley Farm in Somerset.

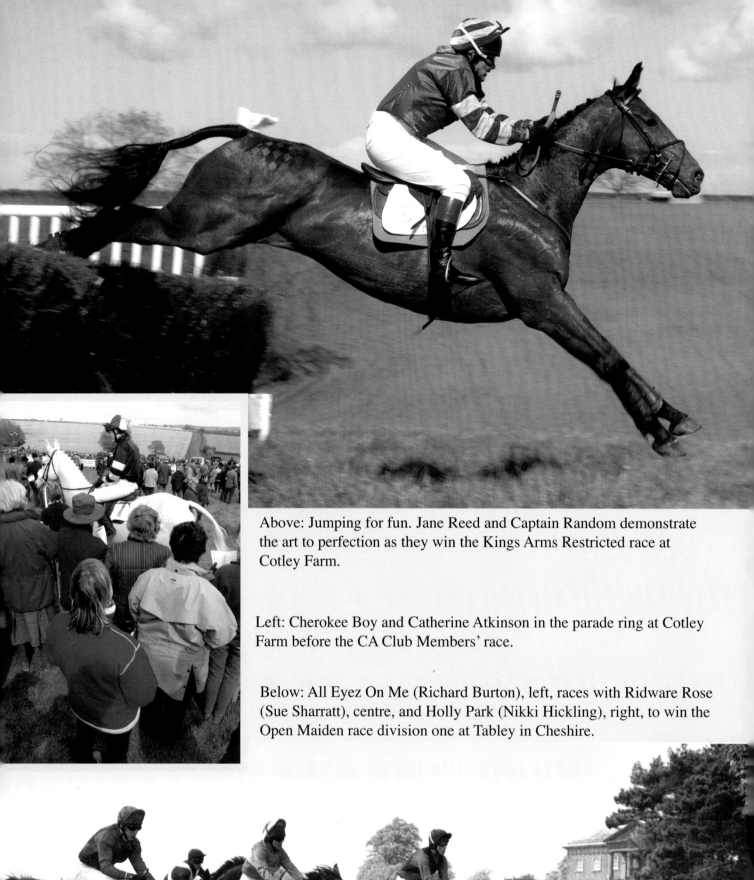

Above: Jumping for fun. Jane Reed and Captain Random demonstrate the art to perfection as they win the Kings Arms Restricted race at Cotley Farm.

Left: Cherokee Boy and Catherine Atkinson in the parade ring at Cotley Farm before the CA Club Members' race.

Below: All Eyez On Me (Richard Burton), left, races with Ridware Rose (Sue Sharratt), centre, and Holly Park (Nikki Hickling), right, to win the Open Maiden race division one at Tabley in Cheshire.

Above: A treble for rider Lee Stephens as Mixed Open winner Rostock leads on the first circuit at Bonvilston with Red Neck (Tim Vaughan), left, Speed Board (Evan Williams), and Berkeley Frontier (Emma Jones), right.

Below: A junior racegoer gets an elevated view of proceedings at Bonvilston in South Wales.

Above: The secretary's welcoming party at Bonvilston. From left: David Burles, secretary Shirley Turner, Chris Bolton, Chris Turner and Julie Tamplin.

Hannah Lewis

Charlotte Owen

William Oakes

Mark Lewis

Above: Just Caramel (Stephen Hughes), left, jumps with Celtic Prince (James Tudor) during the Confined Maiden race at Bonvilston.

Right: St John attendants Aimee Beer (11), left, Victoria Morgan (11) and Charlotte Singleton (12) at Bonvilston.

Below: Collier and Tim Atkinson win the Maiden race at Cotley Farm

Above: Charlotte Owen and Flockmaster glide to victory in the Members' race at Bonvilston.

Left: Andrew and Jill Lowrie receive the trophy from Bonvilston seceretary Shirley Turner, centre, after Clear Away won the Confined Maiden race. Thomas Lowrie (2) proudly displays the racing colours.

Below: Rutherford and Ran Morgan lead the field to win division two of the Maiden race at Mosshouses.

Above: Clarice Starling (Tim Vaughan), far side, jumps with Glastrian (Gareth Perkins), centre, and Beehive Lad (James Price, purple) during the Confined Maiden race at Bonvilston.

Left: Lee Stephens and Silver Castle take the last to win the Intermediate race at Bonvilston.

Right: Emma Jones after the Mixed Open race at Bonvilston.

Above: Gareth Davies hits the deck after Come On Boy refused (but then jumped) with 13 Maiden race runners behind him at Bredwardine.

Above: Mark Wall, left, Rob Hodges (orange) and Gareth Davies after the fourth fence mayhem at Bredwardine and below, the fence steward correctly signals eventual winner Blakeney Hill (James Price) to bypass the last fence.

Above: Richard Burton, right, and James Price head for the changing tent after the nine-race card at Bredwardine.

Lee Stephens

Evan Williams

Steve Hughes

Pollyanna Moore

Above: Highbridge and Patrick Crozier lead throughout to land the Members' race at Bredwardine in Herefordshire.

Right: Upton Adventure and Emma James after winning the Susan Guest Memorial Ladies' Open race at Bredwardine.

Below: Adam Wadlow drives Neminos to the line at Bredwardine to win the Maiden race division two.

Above: Front-running Maiden race winner Terimon's Dream (David Mansell) is pursued by Evanly Miss (Mark Jackson, red) and Ladygal (David Davies), left, and Nessarc (Rhys Hughes, red cap) and Willoughby Flyer (Mark Walters), right, at Bredwardine.

Below: Wild Blade unseats Rhys Jenkins and brings down Cadougold (Michael Keel) at the last fence of the Confined Championship race at Bredwardine.

Above: Frank Morgan of Brightwells, left, presents the trophy to Herby Sharpe and Roger Liddington after Father Tom won the Confined Championship race at Bredwardine.

CHRISTOPHER Sporborg describes himself as a 'retired investment banker pluralist' but he also knows a thing or two about horses. A visit to Brooms Farm, near Bishop's Stortford, reveals spotless stables, secluded meadows and grassy gallops steep enough to stretch the lungs of the toughest racehorse. The Sporborgs have been here in Hertfordshire-Essex border country since 1980 and it was from this yard in 1989 that Freeflow and Christopher's eldest son William were dispatched to tackle the mighty fences at Pardubice in (then) Czechoslovakia finishing a creditable second beaten eight lengths by a horse winning the race for the third time. Those were halcyon days but times have changed. "There are not the good horses in this area that there once were," thinks Christopher who trained his 150th winner in 2002. "Some of the big families are cutting back or have packed up completely. The youngsters are not coming through even though there are the horses to ride – I don't think the interest is there. "I do think the recent idea of holding pony races at professional meetings is a good one but I notice that so far the girls outnumber the boys quite significantly." Walking around the

Christopher Sporborg

yard Christopher points out Will Hill (by Phardante), Neverbepooragain and his favourite Parkers Hills, a grand old stager, now 15 who won his Maiden at Horseheath 10 years ago. In recent years Sporborg horses have arrived at Cottenham on the first day of the season fit and ready to run, landing the opening race for the past two years. Rob Mine, ridden by Andrew Braithwaite, produced the goods in 2003 and The Red Boy, above, again with Braithwaite in the saddle, came up trumps last season after Christopher's younger son Simon retired from race riding due to a combination of weight and work commitments. "I will train a handful of horses this season and we have a very nice youngster named Lightening Conductor who is by Glacial Storm out of Miss Cello by Orchestra. We hope to run him on the opening day at Cottenham in January next year." What would he change given the chance? "I believe that hunt secretaries and committees should be much more innovative and try to organise the area and course planning better. We have short, sharp courses and we have long staying courses which obviously suit different types of horses but this fact doesn't seem to be taken into account."

PPORA awards Stratford upon Avon 2004

Left: The PPORA annual general meeting held before racing at Stratford upon Avon. Chairman Richard Russell and secretary Jeanette Dawson seated on his right.

Right: Jeanette Dawson, PPORA secretary, deals with an enquiry by Martin Harris on the Weatherby Chase table during the annual awards luncheon at Stratford upon Avon.

Above: Torduff Express and Nick Williams take the last fence ahead of the ill-fated Right To Reply (Neil Harris) to win the Intrum Justitia Cup at Stratford upon Avon.

Above: Richard Russell, chairman of the PPORA, left, and John Easden of Intrum Justitia with sucessful rider Nick Williams after the Intrum Justitia Cup won by Torduff Express.

Left: Guignol Du Cochet and Glyn Slade Jones after their Dodson and Horrell PPORA win at Stratford upon Avon.

Above: Over they go. The Intrum Justitia Cup field race into the setting sun at Stratford upon Avon. Leaders are Lord Edwards (Ran Morgan), left, Philtre (Adrian Wintle, red), the grey Bright Approach (Tom Malone) and Mullensgrove (Sarah Phizacklea), far side.

Right: Lucy Bridges is unseated from final-fence leader Polar Champ leaving Colquhoun and Ollie Jackson a simple task to win the Oi Oi Ladies Hunterchase at Stratford upon Avon.

Below: Cantarinho and David Kemp clear the last fence in fine style to land the Weatherbys Chase John Corbet Cup at Stratford upon Avon.

Racing at Bredwardine as the Maiden race runners travel down
towards the river Wye.

Above: Men's Open race winner Well Ted and Julian Pritchard jump upsides Bullfinch (Tim Lane) with a circuit to run at Dingley.

Right: Zoe Turner after her Ladies' Open race win on The Wiley Kalmuck at Dingley.

Below: Intermediate race contenders Carat (Polly Gundry), left, Hedzamarley (Michael Keel) and Slaney Lass (Richard Burton), right, head for the start at scenic Dingley.

Jane Wallace, secretary at Dingley

Nicholas Wain

John Russell

Marc Goldstein

Above: David Barlow makes all on Holding The Fort from Sandy Lark (Andrew Sansome), left, and Ebony Jack (Julian Pritchard), right, to land the Restricted race at Dingley for owner Ian Anderson, pictured right.

Above: Miss Hoity Toity (Andrew Samsome), right, and Tale Bridge (John Russell) lead eventual Members' race winner at Dingley in Northamptonshire.

Below: Andrew Sansome, right, and riding colleagues relax between races during a long hot afternoon at Dingley.

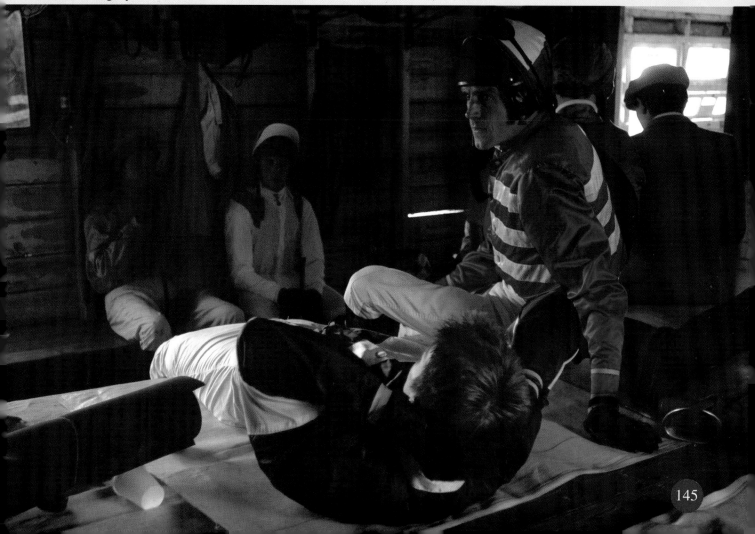

145

Vicky Teal, Lydstep secretary

Tessa Hayes

Kate Diggle

Dai Jones

Above: Richard Woollacott and Timpani lead Ashley Farrant and Cimmaroon during the Intermediate race at Bratton Down in Devon.

Right: Barbara Thomas and Robin Watson, joint secretaries at Bratton Down.

Below: Champion elect Ashley Farrant receives attention from professional physiotherapist Rabbett Slattery before racing at Bratton Down.

Above: Jodie Hughes and Kovach take the last fence to land the Ladie's Open race at Lydstep and, right, unsaddled with second-placed Lucy Rowsell.

Below: Racing down towards the beach at Lydstep. Restricted race winner Newmarket Magic (Dai Jones), left, jumps the last with Its A Handfull (Josh Harris).

Above: Red Neck and Tim Vaughan race with Harppy (Dai Jones) to win the Brightwells Men's Open at Lydstep.

Below: Blackchurch Lass (Jason Cook) and Tiger Rag (Mark Lewis) compete for third place in the Mares' Maiden race at Lydstep.

Above: The Red Neck team line up at Lydstep to receive the Men's Open race prize sponsored by Brightwells.

Above: Senior Welsh rider Dai Jones, riding Clarice Starling, left, congratulates title-chasing Richard Burton on his success aboard Countess Kiri in the Mares' Maiden race at Lydstep.

Below: Maiden race winner Peaceful Bow (Dai Jones) leads the chasing group at Lydstep with Start It Up (Joe Price), left, The Well Lad (Richard Burton, hoops) and Wiston Wizo (Paul Sheldrake) in rear.

Above: Owner and trainer Maggie Stephens with Chief Gale after finishing second at Lydstep in the Members' race.

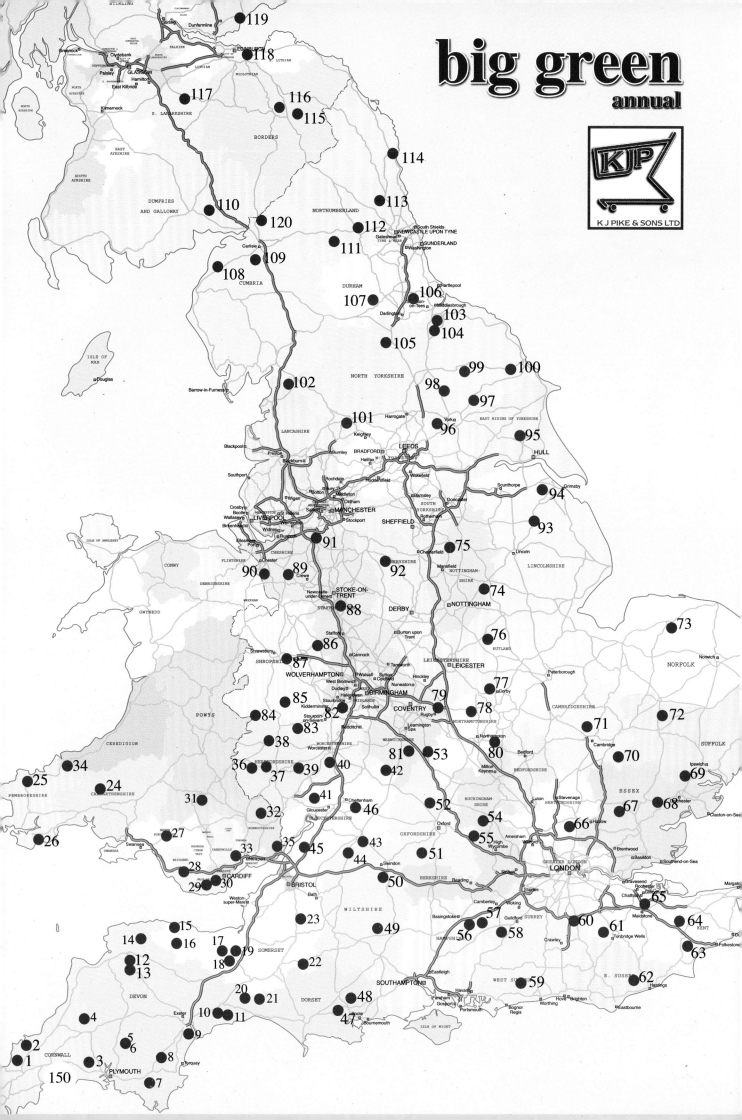

big green annual

2005 course locator

1 Trebudannon	41 Maisemore Park	81 Ashorne
2 Wadebridge	42 Paxford	82 Chaddesley Corbett
3 Great Trethew	43 Siddington	83 Upper Sapey
4 Lifton	44 Didmarton	84 Brampton Bryan
5 Kilworthy	45 Woodford	85 Bitterley
6 Cherrybrook	46 Andoversford	86 Weston Park
7 Flete Park	47 Milborne St Andrew	87 Eyton-on-Severn
8 Buckfastleigh	48 Badbury Rings	88 Sandon
9 Blackforest Lodge	49 Larkhill	89 Alpraham
10 Bishops Court	50 Barbury Castle	90 Eaton Hall
11 Stafford Cross	51 Lockinge	91 Tabley
12 Umberleigh	52 Dunthrop	92 Flagg Moor
13 Vauterhill	53 Mollington	93 Market Rasen
14 Bratton Down	54 Kimble	94 Brocklesby Park
15 Holnicote	55 Kingston Blount	95 Dalton Park
16 Mounsey Hill Gate	56 Hackwood Park	96 Wetherby
17 Cothelstone	57 Tweseldown	97 Whitwell-on-the-Hill
18 Kingston St Mary	58 Peper Harow	98 Easingwold
19 Chipley	59 Parham	99 Duncombe Park
20 Cotley Farm	60 Godstone	100 Charm Park
21 Littlewindsor	61 Penshurst	101 Heslaker Farm
22 Charlton Horethorne	62 Bexhill	102 Whittington
23 Ston Easton	63 Aldington	104 Stainton
24 Erw Lon	64 Charing	104 Hutton Rudby
25 Trecoed	65 Detling	105 Hornby Castle
26 Lydstep	66 Northaw	106 Mordon
27 Pentreclwydau	67 High Easter	107 Witton Castle
28 Laleston	68 Marks Tey	108 Aspatria
29 Ystradowen	69 Higham	109 Dalston
30 Bonvilston	70 Horseheath	110 Lockerbie
31 Llanfrynach	71 Cottenham	111 Hexham
32 llanvapley	72 Ampton	112 Corbridge
33 Rhydygwern	73 Fakenham	113 Tranwell
34 Cilwendeg Farm	74 Thorpe Lodge	114 Alnwick
35 Howick	75 Wellbeck	115 Friars Haugh
36 Bredwardine	76 Garthorpe	116 Mosshouses
37 Garnons	77 Dingley	117 Carluke
38 Colharbour	78 Guilsborough	118 Musselburgh
39 Whitwick Manor	79 Clifton-on-Dunsmore	119 Balcormo Mains
40 Upton-on-Severn	80 Brafield-on-the-Green	120 Netherby

For details of meetings, contact the Point-to-Point Owners and Riders Association on 01227 713080.

151

Above: Like The Buzz and Jason Cook cross the line ahead of Hail Stone (Lee Stephens) to win the Intermediate race at Trecoed.

Right: Sisters Lucy Rowsell, left and Emma Jones find plenty to talk about before the Ladies' Open race at Trecoed.

Below: Lordberniebouffant leads at the last to win the Confined race at Hexham and clinch the northern area title for rider Pauline Robson.

Above: Aljoash and Tim Vaughan set the pace for the Intermediate field at Trecoed in West Wales.

Below: Andrew Hanly leads the Maiden race on Classic Fable followed by Its Mr Blobby (Tim Vaughan) and Portway Sadie (Mark Wall) at Trecoed.

Above: Jane Thornton and Richard Wallace arrive at Trecoed by helicopter to 'support Richard Burton' in his attempt to retain the riders' crown.

Paddy Davies,
Trecoed steward

Dai Miller, Trecoed
secretary

Cynthia Higgon,
Trecoed steward

Brian Lee,
Wales correspondent

Above: Another big turn-out at the popular new course at Trecoed.

Right: Mike Davis presents the owner's prize to rider Tim Underwood and Carolyn Hogg after Mister Pepper won the Men's Open race at Trecoed in West Wales.

Below: Capacoostic and Richard Burton jump into the lead during the Open Maiden race at Trecoed.

Above: Point-to-point enthusiasts Adell Panter, left, Lottie Wood and Holly Williams, right, catch the eye as the temperature rises at Trecoed.

Below: Rathgibbon (James Price), right, jumps with Khatani (Lee Stephens) with a circuit to run in the Men's Open race at Trecoed.

Above: Delaware and Polly Gundry lead the Ladies' Open race followed by Campden Kitty (Jane Williams) and eventual winner Khatani (Lucy Rowsell) at Umberleigh.

Left: James Price (on his stag afternoon/evening) arrives at Umberleigh disguised as 'Dorothy' from *The Wizard of Oz*. The rest of the cast soon joined him on the yellow brick road - but where was Judy Garland?

Below: Waiting in the wings. Having dumped Ken Rixon through the same wing last season, Kingsbridge gives Lucy Bridges the encore 12 months later during the Ladies' Open race.

Above: Riders for the Open Maiden race division two enter the parade ring at Umberleigh on the final day of the 2004 season.

Left: Julie Symons, secretary at Umberleigh, checks the trophies and prizes on offer.

Below: The going turns dusty as the Maiden race field gallop over Barley stubble at Umberleigh.

Above: A huge crowd at Umberleigh on the last day of the 2004 season where Lamerton Quest (James Cole) follows Carvilla (Chris Gordon) during the Open Maiden race.

Below: Having announced his retirement Ashley Farrant, the new champion, heads for the changing tent after his final point-to-point ride.

Left: Summer bedding plants amongst the many stalls and trade stands at Umberleigh.

Above: Jody Sole on Beehive Lad, left, jumps with eventual winner Vitinsel (Jamie Snowden) during division two of the Open Maiden race at Umberleigh.

Below: 'You'll have to speak up" Ashley Farrant gives Polly Gundry's ear a wash out with Champagne as the celebrations begin.

Above: The 2004 season champions line up as numerous cameras record the moment. Trainer David Pipe, left, with ladies' champion Polly Gundry and men's winner Ashley Farrant.

Once again, my sincere thanks to those contributors who have kindly assisted me in this fifth edition of the big green annual: Horse & Hound point-to-point correspondent Carolyn Tanner for her monthly reports, Jeanette Dawson of the PPORA and my fellow photographers.

Special thanks to my son Robert who is the brains behind the operation.